Printing
Industry
Advisory
Committee

Safety in the use of c products in the printi industry

GU01048690

Contents

London:
Her Majesty's
Stationery Office

General enquiries regarding this publication should be
addressed to the Health and Safety Executive at any area
office or to the public enquiry points listed below.

Health and Safety Executive
Library and Information Services
Broad Lane
SHEFFIELD S3 7HQ
Telephone: 0742 752539 Telex: 54556

Health and Safety Executive
Library and Information Services
St Hugh's House
Stanley Precinct
Trinity Road
BOOTLE
Merseyside L20 3QY
Telephone: 051-951 4381 Telex: 628235

Health and Safety Executive
Library and Information Services
Baynards House
1 Chepstow Place
Westbourne Grove
LONDON W2 4TF
Telephone: 01-221 0870
Telex: 25683

ISBN 0 11 883956 X

Introduction to chemical hazards

1   This booklet gives guidance to directors, managers, supervisors, safety representatives and other employees on the safe use of the wide variety of chemical products found in the printing industry.

2   Chemical based processes are fundamental to printing and related activities. When using any chemical product suitable precautions should be taken to minimise risk to health and, in the case of flammable materials, risk of fire and explosion.

3   The guidance begins by summarising how chemicals can affect the body. The range of possible adverse health effects is described under 'inhalation', 'skin and eye contact' and 'ingestion', these being the main ways chemicals enter the body (paragraphs 6 to 19).

4   Safe use of chemical products requires firstly identification, then assessment and finally control of the hazards. A scheme to do this is set out in paragraph 25 and explained more fully in paragraphs 26 to 107. Assessment and control of occupational exposure to chemicals is central to the control of substances hazardous to health framework.

5   The principles outlined in this booklet apply to all printing companies whether large or small. The guidance is not a commentary on legal obligations, but relevant legal requirements are listed in Appendix 1.

Health effects

Inhalation

6   The main way in which gases, vapours and dusts enter the body is by inhalation. Health effects may be restricted to the respiratory tract and lungs, causing irritation or sensitisation (ie development of an allergy to an inhaled chemical), but may extend to other parts of the body if the chemical is absorbed into the bloodstream.

7   Many organic solvents can affect the central nervous system, causing symptoms ranging from mild headaches and nausea to more severe headaches, vomiting or even unconsciousness, depending on the vapour concentration and length of exposure. In other industries deaths have occurred in operations such as cleaning in confined spaces. Other symptoms include changes in behaviour such as loss of concentration and slowed reactions. Exposure to more than one solvent at the same time may accentuate the adverse health effects caused by any one component of the mixture. This possibility should not be ignored as the majority of chemical products used in the printing industry are mixtures. Further information on health effects of solvents can be found in references 1 to 4.

8   The risks to health of inhalation of solvent vapour increase with the volatility and temperature of the solvent. Volatility, or rate of evaporation, is related to boiling pcint - liquids with low boiling points evaporate more quickly than those with high ones. The inhalation risk is also increased when volatile chemical products are used in a confined space, such as below the feed board of a lithographic printing press, or in poorly ventilated work areas. Further risks may arise when products are sprayed or used in such a way that a fine mist is formed; in these circumstances additional control measures may be necessary even if the chemicals concerned are of low volatility.

9   An example of solvent vapour generation can be found in the drying of screen inks, which may contain ketones (such as cyclohexanone), hydrocarbons (such as xylene, white spirit and trimethyl benzenes), and some glycol ethers and their esters. The risk of inhaling vapour from such chemicals is increased when hot air is forced over the printed articles to dry the ink by rapidly evaporating the solvents. To minimise this risk adequate control measures should be applied (paragraphs 45 to 50).

10   In general the health effects of solvent inhalation will depend on the chemical nature of the solvent, its concentration in air and the length of exposure. Table 1 gives some examples of commonly used solvents which, if inhaled, can cause the symptoms described in paragraph 7.

11   In addition to these general symptoms, certain chemicals can cause more specific adverse health effects such as occupational asthma. This may occur through sensitisation so that further contact with even a low concentration of the chemical leads to bronchial irritation. Isocyanates are examples of chemicals which can cause occupational asthma. Within the printing industry they are generally used as partly reacted compounds to make them less volatile. Such prepolymers, however, contain very small quantities of the parent isocyanates; particular control measures are necessary if these materials are heated, sprayed or used in such a way that a fine mist is formed[5].
Table 2 gives examples of chemicals which can cause specific adverse health effects on inhalation. The examples in both Tables 1 and 2 are illustrative only and are not exhaustive.

12   A particular hazard may be present in newspaper pressrooms where rotary letterpress printing is undertaken[9]. A fine mist may be generated by the action of the rollers. Fine mist droplets can be inhaled and reach the lungs. Conventional inks for such newspaper presses are based on mineral oils which contain polynuclear aromatic hydrocarbons, including very small quantities of compounds known or suspected to cause cancer. However, inks based on mineral oils

Table 1   Solvents which can affect the central nervous system when inhaled

The effects on health depend on the particular chemical, its vapour concentration in air and the length of exposure - see paragraph 7.

Type/name of chemical	Examples of use
Ketones, eg cyclohexanone, methyl ethyl ketone (MEK)	Gravure inks (MEK) Screen inks (cyclohexanone) Blanket restorers (MEK) Cleaning solvents (MEK)
Alcohols, eg ethyl alcohol (as in industrial methylated spirits, IMS), n-propyl alcohol, isopropyl alcohol	Flexographic inks Gravure inks Fount solutions
Esters, eg ethyl acetate, butyl acetate	Flexographic inks Gravure inks
Aromatic hydrocarbons, eg toluene, xylene, trimethyl benzenes	Gravure inks (toluene) Screen inks (xylene, trimethyl benzenes)

Table 2   Specific effects of certain chemicals when inhaled

The specific health effects are in addition to those in paragraph 7.

The effects on health depend on the particular chemical, its vapour concentration in air and the length of exposure and may be immediate (acute) or long term (chronic).

Type/name of chemical	Examples of use	Specific health effects
Chlorinated hydrocarbons eg 1,1,1-trichloroethane[6]	Cleaning rollers and cylinders	Cardiac arrhythmias (high concentration) Affect liver and kidneys on long term exposure
Ammonium hydroxide	Dyeline printing	Irritation of the respiratory tract (as ammonia vapour)
Certain glycol ethers,[7,8] eg EGME, EGEE (see notes)	Non-aqueous litho plate making Flexographic inks Screen inks Gravure inks	Affects bone marrow (EGME, high concentration) Reproductive damage (in experimental animals at low concentration)
Prepolymers containing trace isocyanate, eg TDI, MDI (see notes)	Lacquers, primers, adhesives	Irritation of the throat and upper respiratory tract (high concentration) Sensitisation causing asthma (see paragraph 11)

Notes

EGME: ethylene glycol monomethyl ether, 2-methoxy ethanol (methyl cellosolve, etc)

EGEE: ethylene glycol monoethyl ether, 2-ethoxy ethanol (cellosolve, etc)

Acetate derivatives of glycol ethers are considered to have the same toxic properties as the parent compounds

Glycol ethers can also be readily absorbed through the skin - see Table 3

TDI: toluene di-isocyanate

MDI: methylene di-isocyanate

which contain lower levels of polynuclear aromatic hydrocarbons are now available.

13 Solvents such as acetone, methyl ethyl ketone (MEK), and isopropyl alcohol (Table 1) are highly flammable; precautions in storage and handling of highly flammable liquids are summarised in paragraphs 64 to 76.

14 In general, chemical products with inhalation hazards can be used safely provided that appropriate precautionary measures (paragraphs 43 to 55) are adopted.

Skin and eye contact

15 Many chemicals are harmful by skin contact[10]. The eyes are particularly vulnerable. In general, the skin is a good chemical barrier (except where there are cuts or wounds) and adverse effects are often limited to the skin itself. However many organic solvents (for example those in Table 1) can remove the skin's natural oils and prolonged exposure can cause drying or flaking, which reduces the skin's effectiveness as a protective barrier. Some chemicals, for example glycol ethers, can pass through the skin and so affect other body organs.

16 Contact dermatitis may result from exposure to certain chemicals, and can range from mild to severe irritant (non-allergic) dermatitis. It can occur even after only one or two exposures.

17 Some chemicals, even though they do not have any direct irritant effect on the skin, can cause an allergic contact dermatitis through sensitisation. Such a reaction can occur suddenly even though a person may have worked with the chemical for many years without experiencing problems. Once sensitised, the same skin response can occur on exposure to very small amounts of the chemical.

18 In general damage to the skin or eyes decreases with dilution and increases with prolonged contact.

Table 3 gives examples of chemicals that can cause skin or eye contact hazards. Measures to minimise skin and eye contact are given in paragraphs 56 to 62.

Ingestion

19 Although ingestion is a less usual occupational route of uptake into the body the hazard should not be ignored. Lead poisoning, for example, can be caused by ingesting small quantities of the metal over a prolonged period. Such ingestion may be caused by repeated eating of food or smoking with hands contaminated by lead dust. Such lack of attention to basic hygiene can also lead to ingestion of other hazardous chemicals.

Exposure limits

20 Guidance Note EH40[12] lists exposure limits for a wide variety of chemicals used at work. It should be consulted for further information. Exposure limits are not sharp demarcations between safe and unsafe conditions, and they do not take into account any additive effects on exposure to mixtures of chemicals. Exposure to all chemicals should be kept as low as is reasonably practicable, primarily by applying process controls[13]. Absence of a particular substance from the list does not imply that the substance is not toxic.

Fire and explosion

21 Combustible material and sources of ignition are present in all printing premises. Flammable liquids are widely used. Some sources of ignition, such as a flame from a welding torch, a hot surface, or a spark from an electrical motor or switchgear, are obvious. Others, such as static discharge (see paragraph 74), may not be immediately apparent.

Table 3 Chemicals with particular skin or eye contact hazards

Damage to the skin and eyes generally decreases with dilution and increases on prolonged contact (sensitisation effects excepted).

Type/name of chemical	Examples of use	Health effect
Strong acids, eg concentrated nitric and sulphuric acids, hydrofluoric acid	Etching, engraving, platemaking, certain photographic reproduction systems, correction of litho plates (hydrofluoric acid)	Skin burns and blisters. Burns with concentrated hydrofluoric acid are very severe. Eye damage
Strong alkalis, eg concentrated sodium hydroxide or potassium hydroxide	Cleaning of screens in screen printing	Skin burns. Very severe eye damage
Acrylates or methacrylates[11]	UV and electron beam cured inks, varnishes and lacquers	Irritation and sensitisation
Dichromates, eg ammonium, potassium and sodium dichromates	Litho platemaking, gravure cylinder preparation, photo-engraving, photographic bleaches	Very corrosive. In high concentrations can cause deep ulcers
Glycol ethers[7,8]	As in Table 2	Readily absorbed through the skin. Effects as in Table 2

22 Solid or liquid combustible materials can be ignited if heated sufficiently to give off flammable concentrations of gases. The amount of heat needed to ignite solids is often substantial, unless they are present as a fine dust. An indication of the flammability of a liquid is its flash point (the temperature at which a liquid gives off flammable vapour which can explode or catch fire if exposed to a source of ignition). The greater the volatility, the more readily flammable vapour is produced and the lower is the flash point. Ignition can occur only when the concentration of vapour is within a certain range, defined by the lower and upper explosive limits. These limits are usually expressed as a percentage concentration in air.

23 Once a fire has started its severity depends on the nature and quantity of combustible material present. Small quantities of any flammable liquid or a liquefied flammable gas (eg LPG) can produce a relatively large volume of flammable vapour, and so present a serious hazard if mishandled. Special circumstances can further increase the hazard. An example is confinement of a combustion process so that there is a substantial pressure rise, leading to an explosion.

24 Precautionary measures to minimise risk of fire and explosion are set out in paragraphs 64 to 76.

Using chemicals safely

General scheme for safe use

25 Print company managers should take the following steps to identify hazards, assess risks and develop effective control measures for all chemicals and processes, whether in use or being considered for use in the industry:

(a) collect health and safety information;

(b) select the least hazardous product;

(c) assess risks in relation to site conditions;

(d) provide control measures for hazards associated with:

- inhalation
- skin and eye contact
- ingestion
- fire and explosion

(e) make arrangements for:

- storage, handling and transport
- spillage control
- disposal
- maintenance work
- housekeeping
- first aid

(f) instruct and train personnel;

(g) maintain records and review control measures.

Safety representatives should be involved in identifying the hazards, assessing the risks and determining the necessary control measures. The organisation and arrangements for safe use of chemical products should be included in the written company health and safety policy statements[14,15].

Collection of health and safety information

26 Users should make sure that they have safety information on **all** existing chemical products and processes used on their premises. New knowledge may require improved safety measures. Information should be kept up-to-date through regular contact with suppliers and by referring to other sources, eg HSE *Toxic Substances Bulletin* published twice yearly and HSC bimonthly *Newsletter*.

27 The supplier has a responsibility to ensure that the products provided are safe and without risk to health when properly used. The supplier should also provide information on how to use the products safely.

28 Before introducing a product or process new to the company all relevant safety information should be obtained from the supplier (and other sources as necessary). This also applies when using trial samples and when suppliers representatives are demonstrating their products on site.

29 Suppliers may provide health and safety information by means of:

(a) safety data sheets; and

(b) warning labels on product containers and on the packages in which they are transported; and

(c) notes of other technical details as necessary.

30 Guidance on the content of suppliers safety data sheets for the printing industry has been prepared[16] and users should check that all relevant information is included. General guidance for all industries on the need for safety data sheets, together with their content and proper use is also available[17].

31 The statutory warning labels on product containers as supplied use the following classifications: explosive, oxidising, extremely flammable (flashpoint below 0°C), highly flammable (flashpoint below 21°C), flammable (flashpoint between 21° and 55°C), very toxic, toxic, corrosive, harmful, and irritant. The label should include certain risk and safety phrases which give the user immediate and concise information[18]. The advice given on the label, however, does not provide a full safety assessment of the product and may not identify particular products as being subject to specific controls. An example is highly flammable liquids - see paragraph 64. In addition some chemical products are not required to be labelled by law but appropriate precautions are still necessary if they are to be used safely.

32 Thus an adequate assessment of the risks cannot be made unless health and safety data is obtained for all products used whether or not the product containers carry warning labels.

33 As working conditions vary from one company to another the information provided on data sheets and labels may not answer all the users queries, in which case the user should, in the first instance, ask the supplier for further assistance. Some other sources of advice are listed in Appendix 2.

Selection of the least hazardous product

34 When selecting products for particular applications care should be taken to choose those which present the lowest overall hazard. Sometimes the ready availability of safer alternatives leads to an acceptance throughout the industry that certain highly toxic chemicals need never be used. An example is benzene, which can cause cancer.

35 Sometimes risk in use can be reduced by changing the physical form of the product. Pastes or liquids, for example, are likely to be of lower risk in use than powdery solids. When choosing the least hazardous product fire and explosion as well as health hazards should be considered.

Assessment of risks

36 The information obtained about the chosen product (or process) should be considered in the light of how and where the product is or will be used. Risks should be assessed in order to determine the necessary control measures.

37 To make the assessment the following questions should be answered:

(a) is there a health hazard? If so, would it be through inhalation, ingestion and/or skin contact, and what is the potential extent of exposure?

(b) is there a fire or explosion hazard?

(c) are special storage, handling and disposal procedures required?

(d) will maintenance personnel be at risk?

(e) what emergency action should be taken in, for example, the event of a spillage?

(f) could any airborne emission from the plant cause harm or annoyance to persons outside the company?

38 A senior person should be made responsible for this assessment. This person should have a good practical knowledge of the industry and be familiar with the daily working routine of the company. In larger companies a team of people may be involved which could include the production manager, safety officer, and medical adviser. Safety representatives should also be involved.

39 Where the assessment shows that existing control measures for chemical products in use are inadequate, urgent remedial action should be taken.

40 Before a chemical product new to the company is used for the first time the responsible person (paragraph 38) should review the information collected and consider whether the existing control measures are sufficient and whether the operatives have been adequately instructed and trained (paragraphs 42 to 99). Improved control measures and additional instruction and training should be provided as necessary.

41 If the requirements for safe use are satisfied, the product should be authorised for initial use. In some cases such authorisation may be conditional upon satisfactory results of atmospheric sampling to test the effectiveness of the control measures. In these circumstances operatives should be provided with, and should wear, suitable protective equipment until effectiveness is demonstrated.

Provision of control measures

42 Control measures should minimise exposure to chemicals by inhalation, skin or eye contact, or ingestion. Wherever practicable this should be achieved by engineering control at source, for example, local exhaust ventilation, together with other measures such as use of pumped and piped systems. Even so, use of personal protective clothing and equipment may sometimes be essential. In all cases workrooms should be well ventilated (for example, by mechanical ventilation systems) and appropriate safe systems of work should be adopted.

Inhalation

43 Some printing processes give off fume or vapour which may present a health hazard or be objectionable to operators. The source of the fume or vapour may be inks, lacquers, press chemicals, solvent based developers, or strong acids or alkalis. Sometimes dust may be generated, for example at slitters and folders of web fed presses or in the use of spray powders.

44 The measures taken should ensure that exposure to levels of potentially harmful airborne contaminants does not exceed current exposure limits and is in any case as low as is reasonably practicable. This may be achieved by one or more of the following:

(a) enclosure of the process;

(b) local exhaust ventilation;

(c) respiratory protective equipment.

Wherever practicable, the first two should be adopted.

Ventilation control

45 The design of ventilation systems is a specialised matter on which expert advice should be sought and is beyond the scope of this guidance[19]. In practice the ventilation measures to control inhalation and fire/explosion hazards are combined and factors such as the quantity of materials used, frequency of use, volatility, flash point and explosive limit should be considered in addition to the exposure limits. The views of operators and appointed safety representatives should be taken into account as they have first hand experience of the processes and working conditions.

46 The following points may, however, be helpful in designing local exhaust ventilation systems:

(a) extraction hoods should be positioned as close as practicable to the point of generation of fume, vapour or dust, and should enclose the source to the greatest practicable extent;

(b) the ducting should be of adequate diameter, and as short and as straight as practicable. Bends should be of gentle radius and 'T' section junctions should be avoided;

(c) the system should be designed and constructed to take account of any flammable properties of the chemicals extracted (see paragraph 64 to 76); and

(d) the system should vent to a safe place in the open air in such a manner that neighbours are not subject to nuisance. If vents are poorly sited discharged vapour may enter buildings through doors, windows, roof spaces or intakes to air conditioning systems. In some cases the air may need to be cleaned before it is discharged to the outside atmosphere.

47 General workroom ventilation needs an input of air to replace that extracted, and should be designed to achieve uniform air distribution within the workroom. As a means of controlling contaminants air should flow away from operators and past source(s) of fume or vapour. Because large volumes of air have to be moved, using general ventilation as a control method leads to an expensive waste of workroom heating. It is more effective and cheaper to control the contaminant at source either by enclosing the process or by providing a local exhaust ventilation system.

Examples of enclosure and ventilation control

48 Inks used in flexographic and gravure printing contain volatile solvents. To reduce exposure, ink ducts and supply vessels should be enclosed and vapour from drying tunnels should be vented to a safe place outside the premises. Local exhaust ventilation should be provided as necessary at printing stations. Additional precautions will be required to control the fire risk - see paragraphs 64 to 76.

49 Automatic enclosed lithographic plate processing systems using volatile solvents should be provided with local exhaust ventilation. Automatic systems are preferable to manual processing in order to minimise contact with chemicals. Where manual processing of solvent based plate systems is undertaken, down-draught tables that draw air and vapour towards the floor and then to an exhaust vent terminating in a safe place in the open air are recommended.

50 Drying ovens on automatic or semi-automatic screen printing lines using solvent based inks should have effective means of venting solvent laden air to a safe position outside the premises. Screens should be cleaned and reclaimed in totally enclosed systems or under conditions that ensure proper control of solvent vapour in the operator's breathing zone. This may involve carefully removing ink from the screen by hand under local exhaust ventilation and drying the screen after using screen wash and before jetting with water.

51 Darkrooms should have mechanical ventilation to ensure safe and comfortable working conditions. A ventilation rate of 10 to 15 air changes per hour may be necessary. Ventilation may be provided at the required rate by a suitable extractor fan mounted in an outside wall, but it is important to provide an air inlet otherwise the desired ventilation rate may not be achieved. Air inlet(s) should be at low level and may contain a filter to prevent entry of dust. Air inlets can be made light-tight by providing downward sloping louvres on both sides.

52 The use of enclosed or local exhaust ventilation systems in processes involving isocyanate prepolymers in the printing and printed packaging industries is considered in other PIAC guidance[5]. Three examples of plant where such control measures are generally required are application units, drying tunnels and laminating nips.

53 Ozone produced, for example, by ultraviolet curing units should be removed by mechanical extraction and vented at a suitable point in the open air[11,20]. Mechanical extraction may also be required for cooling purposes.

Respiratory protective equipment

54 Where adequate engineering control at source is impracticable, for example, during some maintenance work, respiratory protective equipment should be used. Respirators may have to be worn, for example, when changing ammonia containers or when dealing with a spillage of ammonia solution used in dyeline printing.

55 Proper uses of respirators requires:

(a) careful selection of the correct respirator for the job. Canister-type respirators, for example, may be used to protect against inhalation of vapour. The canister should be selected so that it effectively adsorbs the chemical vapour concerned. Such respirators, however, should never be used in confined spaces, where breathing apparatus (which enables the wearer to breathe from an independent source of clean air) is required. The advice of the suppliers should be followed. To protect against inhalation of asbestos fibres or lead dust or fume, only suitable respirators approved by HSE should be used. A list of approved respirators is published annually[21];

(b) care in ensuring that the respirator fits the wearer and that there is a proper seal between the face and the respirator;

(c) full training of wearers and their supervisors in how to use respirators correctly and what the limitations of such equipment are; and

(d) regular cleaning, inspection and maintenance.

Further guidance on the selection, use and maintenance of respiratory protective equipment is available in British Standard 4275[22].

Skin and eye contact

56 Measures should be taken to minimise skin and eye contact. Skin contact can be reduced by good plant design, for example, by using automatic processing equipment that incorporates means of pumping chemicals from preparation vessels to the points of use. In addition to health and safety considerations, such equipment can lead to considerable savings in usage of chemicals.

57 Where automated procedures are not practicable, safe systems of work are particularly important. Protective clothing such as gloves, aprons and eye/face protection should be provided and used as necessary. Consideration should also be given to use of suitable footwear.

58 Protective gloves and aprons should be made of suitable material that is resistant to the chemicals used. Gloves should be rinsed thoroughly under running water before they are removed. In practice use of disposable gloves may be more convenient. Protective clothing should be regularly inspected and discarded if there are signs of wear. Protective and personal clothing should not be stored in the same locker; separate facilities should be provided.

59 Neat solvents should not be used to remove dirt or grease from the skin. Proprietary skin cleaning preparations should be used.

60 Whenever there is a risk of splashing, for example when bulk chemicals are decanted, protective goggles or face shields should be worn. It is advisable, in areas where chemicals are regularly used, to provide eye wash bottles or some other means of washing out the eyes as a first aid measure in case of accident.

61 Goggles or face shields used for protection against chemical splashing should be to British Standard 2092-C specification ('C' denoting suitability for use against liquid splashes or droplets)[23].

62 Protective clothing should be worn during mixing or other preparatory work and during cleaning procedures, as well as in the course of production.

Ingestion

63 To avoid ingestion of chemicals good personal hygiene is important. Hands should be thoroughly washed immediately after contact with chemicals and before eating, smoking, drinking or using toilet facilities. Eating, drinking and smoking should be forbidden in work areas where chemicals are used; if necessary a separate area should be set aside for these purposes. Chemicals should not be kept in cups, bottles or other containers where they may be mistaken for food or drink.

Fire and explosion

64 Flammable liquids always present a fire or explosion hazard and their storage and use should be strictly controlled[24]. It is important to check the flash point in the suppliers safety data sheets rather than rely on the supply labels (paragraph 31) as the Highly Flammable Liquids and Liquefied Petroleum Gases Regulations, which govern storage and use of highly flammable liquids, apply to all liquids with a flashpoint below 32°C.

65 Small quantities of highly flammable liquids should be kept in closed vessels within a container of fire resisting construction, for example, a metal cabinet or cupboard. The maximum total quantity that may be stored in a workroom in this manner is 50 litres. Such storage arrangements should be adequate for many letterpress, litho and screen printers who should be able to keep stocks of highly flammable liquids to below 50 litres.

66 Larger quantities should be stored in:

(a) a safe position in the open air, protected from direct sunlight and from vandals; or

(b) a single storey storeroom detached from other buildings and situated in a safe place; or

(c) a storeroom of fire resisting construction[25] within a building.

Storerooms should have adequate ventilation, eg a number of air bricks at high and low levels in an outside wall, and a sill or lip at the door to contain leakage. Potential sources of ignition, such as electric lights and switches, should be excluded or be of Zone 2 standard[26,27].

67 Within the printing industry highly flammable liquids are often supplied in drums, for which storage as in (a) above is preferred.

68 Storage areas, cabinets and cupboards should be labelled to indicate the presence of highly flammable liquids. Other combustible materials should not, of course, be kept in such storage facilities. Decanting or mixing should never be undertaken in a storeroom. Whenever practicable highly flammable liquids should be piped from the storage location to the point of use. More detailed guidance on storage of highly flammable liquids is available in reference 28.

69 Flexographic, gravure or other printing areas in which significant quantities of highly flammable liquids are used should be well ventilated and provided as necessary with fire separation from storage areas and other parts of the building.

70 Wherever highly flammable liquids are used the risk of ignition of flammable vapour should be assessed. Motors, switches, lights and other electrical equipment should be sited in a safe place where dangerous concentrations of flammable vapour cannot accumulate, or should be designed to the appropriate standard to prevent ignition of flammable vapour[26,27].

71 Where enclosure and/or exhaust ventilation are used to control flammable vapour, the enclosure and ducting should be fire resistant. Electric motors driving extraction fans should not be in the path of the vapour. The design of exhaust ventilation systems should follow the principles in paragraphs 45 and 46.

72 Drying tunnels should be mechanically ventilated to prevent flammable vapour exceeding 25% of the lower explosive limit, and should have explosion relief. Air flow switches or other means should be provided to detect inadequate air extraction. Explosions have occurred, for example, in heat set dryers on web offset presses when the web was usesd as a wiper during wash up. Dryer ventilation fans should be interlocked with the press drive so they continue to operate during press make-ready, running and wash up procedures. Further information can be found in references 29 and 30.

73 Proprietary safety containers are recommended for the dispensing and application of small quantities of flammable liquids. Rags or wipers that have been used with flammable materials should be put in metal bins with well fitting lids. Obviously a no smoking rule should be enforced in any areas where highly flammable liquids are stored or used.

74 Operations like pouring, mixing and pumping of organic solvents such as toluene (a highly flammable liquid) can generate static electricity. Many serious fires have been caused by static. It can be controlled by providing and maintaining efficient earthing arrangements, using antistatic additives, eliminating free

fall of liquids during transfer operations and limiting pumping speeds[31,32]. Control of static is a matter on which specialist advice should be taken; further details are outside the scope of this guidance.

75 Other matters that are also outside the scope of this guidance, but on which advice is available elsewhere, are storage and use of LPG[33,34] and gas flood fire fighting systems[35].

76 The local Fire Authority should be consulted on such matters as fire alarms, fire fighting equipment and means of escape in case of fire. Where the highly flammable liquids kept are also petroleum mixtures, a licence is required from the local petroleum licensing authority.

Other arrangements

Storage, handling and transport

77 Storage and handling facilities should be provided both for bulk materials in central stores and for chemicals used in work areas (see paragraphs 64 to 76 for particular requirements for flammable liquids). Storage areas should be cool, secure and well ventilated, and should have means of containing spilled liquid. Means should also be provided to transfer chemicals safely from central stores to workrooms, for example by using carboy trucks and Winchester carriers.

78 If different classes of chemicals come into contact with each other toxic gases may be generated, or there may be a fire or even a violent explosion. Examples of incompatible chemicals that should never be allowed to mix are:

(a) organic solvents with strong oxidising agents;

(b) strong acids with bleaches.

Such incompatible chemicals should be physically separated in storage to prevent accidental contact. The suppliers health and safety data sheets should include information on conditions for safe storage. General guidance on the safe storage of packaged chemical products is available in reference 36.

79 When handling any chemical product always;

(a) seal the container after use;

(b) avoid spray application;

(c) avoid skin contact; and

(d) use the minimum quantity.

Used cleaning rags or wipers should be stored in sealed, clearly marked containers and should be removed from the workroom at the end of the day.

80   All chemical containers should be clearly labelled. No more than one shift's supply of chemical products should be kept in workrooms.

Spillage control

81   All chemical spillages should be dealt with promptly. As a general rule, small spillages should be mopped up with absorbent rags or paper and the area should then be washed. Larger spillages should be contained using inert absorbent materials or sand, to stop the liquids (particularly organic solvents) entering the drains. Waste rags and absorbing materials should not be thrown into rubbish bins; they should be disposed of as outlined in paragraph 79. Appropriate protective clothing should be used when dealing with spillages.

82   Simple measures, such as use of spillage retention trays, should be taken to minimise the consequences of spillages. The preparation of a spillage 'pack', which should be kept readily available, is also recommended. It should contain a selection of absorbent materials, suitable protective clothing, appropriate canister respirators, emergency instructions etc. Some products (eg those containing isocyanate[5]) will require specific decontamination procedures or other specialist treatment. Further guidance on the action to be taken in the event of chemical spillage within workrooms is available in reference 37.

83   In exceptional circumstances quantities of chemicals stored may be sufficiently large that, in the event of fire, explosion, or major spillage serious danger might occur to people on or outside the premises, or to the environment. In such cases a detailed emergency plan should be drawn up, in consultation with the local authority and the emergency services. Specific requirements may apply if more than certain quantities of particular chemicals are present[38,39].

Disposal

84   Waste materials should be disposed of in accordance with local authority regulations. Discharge to drain of organic solvents or effluents containing heavy metals is not permitted. Waste products of this nature should be collected, labelled and stored in a safe place until arrangements can be made for specialist treatment off-site. Advice can be obtained from the supplier and from the local authority.

85   The disposal arrangements should ensure that incompatible chemicals (paragraph 78) are kept apart. In one instance a violent explosion ensued when spent developer containing organic solvents was inadvertently mixed with concentrated nitric acid, a strong oxidising agent. The spent developer was being bulked for disposal in a drum which had not been washed out and which still contained some acid.

Maintenance work

86   Maintenance personnel may, at times, be exposed to risks which are not normally encountered by process workers. For instance, during cleaning or maintenance operations on equipment, there may be excessive exposure to chemicals or solvent vapour. In these circumstances suitable respirators (paragraphs 54 and 55) and protective clothing should be provided. If the suitability is in doubt the supplier should be consulted.

87   Accidents have occurred when process workers have been unaware that maintenance work was being carried out in their area. The system of work should ensure that plant is made safe for access by maintenance staff. Process workers and maintenance staff should be fully instructed in the precautionary measures required. The system of work should also include safe handing back of plant from maintenance to operating staff.

88   A formal permit to work system is essential when danger can arise during maintenance work on plant incorporating pumps, pipelines, storage and mixing vessels. Particular hazards can arise when cleaning tanks and mixing vessels[40,41]. Reference 40 includes an example of a written permit to work system.

89   Maintenance work outside the building should not be forgotten, for example, plant with exhaust ventilation should be formally shut down when maintenance work is to be undertaken in areas where the ventilation ducts terminate.

90   Asbestos may be present in insulating material around boilers, calorifiers, pipework and lead melting/casting pots, as well as in insulation board, roofing and guttering materials, and in sprayed coatings in roof spaces or on steelwork. Strict control measures should be applied whenever asbestos containing materials are disturbed. Where asbestos containing materials are likely to be present the procedure in reference 42 should be followed.

Housekeeping

91   Workrooms should be cleaned and tidied and waste bins emptied regularly. Vacuum cleaning is preferable, but if a suitable vacuum cleaner is not available, floors should be damped down before sweeping to reduce dust levels.

92   Tidy housekeeping and orderly storage of inks, thinners, cleaning solvents etc will help secure safe working conditions (and contribute to efficient production).

First aid

93 Should there be an accident prompt action is essential. First aid equipment should be kept close to where the chemical products are being used. Any further exposure should be prevented and areas of the body that have come into contact with the chemical should be washed thoroughly with water. Contaminated clothing should be removed and cleaned before re-use.

94 Simple first aid procedures should be set out in the suppliers data sheets or on the company's own internal data sheets (paragraph 97). Further details of first aid requirements can be found in reference 43. If there is any doubt whatsoever, obtain medical advice as soon as possible and show the doctors the safety data sheets for the chemical products involved.

Instruction and training of personnel

95 All people associated with the use of chemical products, including first aid personnel and line managers responsible for areas in which chemical products are used, should be adequately trained in how to handle chemical products safely. If the chemicals used are especially hazardous or the necessary expertise is not available in-house, external organisations may have to be used to train managers and operatives.

96 Training programmes should be updated as necessary. New entrants to the company should be given full training as soon as possible. Instruction and training should be reinforced from time to time.

97 Operatives and safety representatives should have access to the information in the suppliers safety data sheets. However the format of these sheets may not be considered adequate for the conditions operating within the company. In such circumstances the senior person, or the company safety team (paragraph 38), should compile internal information sheets to give more specific details on use, control measures, and emergency action. Naturally such internal information sheets should not omit or minimise the health hazards of the chemicals concerned.

98 Important handling precautions, such as the use of face shields, gloves and aprons, together with any essential first aid measures, can be prominently displayed by means of placards. Where appropriate the standard format and colours for safety signs should be followed[44,45]. Issue of pocket-size cards for ready reference can be a useful way of providing each employee with information.

99 Although the employer has the primary responsibility for ensuring that working conditions are safe and without risk to health, all employees should take reasonable care for the health and safety of themselves and of others who may be affected by their acts or omissions at work. Employees should not intentionally or recklessly interfere with or misuse anything provided in the interests of health and safety.

Maintenance of records and review of control measures

100 It is recommended that a chemical register should be maintained listing all chemical products authorised by the company for use. It should include all process chemicals and any other chemical products used for maintenance and cleaning. Products should not be entered on the register or purchased in quantity until they have been assessed for safety (as well as for technical merit).

101 The register should contain the following information:

(a) chemical name or trade name;

(b) selected alternative product if any;

(c) supplier;

(d) container type and size, storage conditions;

(e) maximum quantity per order, minimum re-order level;

(f) maximum quantity permitted on site;

(g) where used in the company;

(h) suppliers safety data sheet, and location of copies;

(i) internal information sheet where appropriate;

(j) company's technical assessment where appropriate.

102 One way in which this information can be used is to help buyers ensure that only chemical products which have been adequately assessed are purchased. It can also ensure that specifications are not accidentally changed. Purchase of large containers, for instance, may pose added risks in their handling, storage and use unless suitable facilities are available. A systematic ordering system should ensure that stocks are held at reasonable levels that are compatible with the storage facilities on site.

103 All control measures should be reviewed frequently to ensure their effectiveness. Company safety committees can provide a forum within which management and safety representatives can discuss this matter.

104 Air extraction systems should be cleaned regularly and their effectiveness checked by measuring air flow rates and comparing the results with specifications. All other safety equipment, such as fire extinguishers, respirators, first aid equipment, protective clothing etc should be checked and inspected regularly.

105 Supervision should be adequate to ensure that on a day to day basis safe working practices are followed and personal protective equipment is properly used.

106 All injuries, dangerous incidents, reports of ill health and 'near misses' should be recorded and thoroughly investigated. Preparation of a brief written report is recommended. This should include any necessary improvements in the control measures to prevent recurrence.

107 Certain injuries, dangerous occurrences and cases of disease have to be reported to the enforcing authority in writing (and also directly by telephone for the most serious incidents). The enforcing authority for printing undertakings is usually the Health and Safety Executive. It is usually the responsibility of the employer or the person controlling the premises to make this report. Further details can be found in free leaflets[46,47] and in other guidance[48].

Appendix 1 Legal references

Factories Act 1961   1961 Ch. 34

Health and Safety at Work etc Act 1974   1974 Ch. 37

Control of Pollution Act 1974   1974 Ch. 40

Petroleum (Consolidation) Act 1928   1928 Ch. 32

Petroleum (Mixtures) Order 1929   S.R & O 993

Highly Flammable Liquids and Liquefied Petroleum Gases Regulations 1972   SI 917

Protection of Eyes Regulations 1974   SI 1681

Safety Representatives and Safety Committee Regulations 1977 and associated Approved Code of Practice *Safety Representatives and Safety Committees*   SI 500

Classification Packaging and Labelling of Dangerous Substances Regulations 1984 and associated Approved Code of Practice *Classification and Labelling of*

Substances Dangerous for Supply and/or Conveyance by Road and associated Authorised and Approved Lists   SI 1222

Health and Safety (First Aid) Regulations 1981   SI 917

Control of Lead at Work Regulations 1980 and associated Approved Code Practice *Control of Lead at Work*   SI 1248

The Safety Signs Regulations 1980   SI 1471

The Notification of Installations Handling Hazardous Substances Regulations 1982   SI 1357

Control of Industrial Major Accident Hazard Regulations 1984   SI 1902

The Reporting of Injuries, Diseases and Dangerous Occurrences Regulations 1985   SI 2023

Approved Code of Practice, *Work with Asbestos Insulation and Asbestos Coating* revised February 1985

Appendix 2 Sources of information and advice

The Health and Safety Executive incorporates HM Factory Inspectorate and the Employment Medical Advisory Service. The full Bootle headquarters address is given on page (ii) of this booklet. Look under Health and Safety Executive in the telephone directory for your local area office.

The Printing National Industry Group and the Secretariat to the Printing Industry Advisory Committee are based at the Health and Safety Executive, Chancel House, Neasden Lane, London NW10 2UD.

Other useful addresses

British Printing Industries Federation (BPIF)
11 Bedford Row
London WC1R 4DX
01-242 6904

Society of Master Printers of Scotland (SMPS)
Edinburgh House
3/11 North Andrews Street
Edinburgh EH2 1JU
031-557 3600

Society of Graphical and Allied Trades (SOGAT)
274/288 London Road
Hadleigh
Essex SS7 2DE
0702 554111

National Graphical Association (NGA)
Graphic House
63/68 Bromham Road
Bedford MK40 2AG
0234 51521

British Federation of Printing Machinery and Supplies
(BFPMS)
3 Plough Place
Fetter Lane
London EC4A 1AL
01-583 7433

Society of British Printing Ink Manufacturers (SBPIM)
Randalls Road
Leatherhead
Surrey KT22 7RU
0372 378628

Display Producers and Screen Printers Association
(DPSPA)
243 Grays Inn Road
London WC1X 8RB
01-837 2275

Newspaper Publishers Association (NPA)
6 Bouverie Street
London EC4Y 8AY
01-583 8132

Newspaper Society (NS)
Bloomsbury House
Bloomsbury Square
74 - 77 Great Russell Street
London WC1B 3DA
01-636 7014

Printing Industries Research Association (PIRA)
Randalls Road
Leatherhead
Surrey KT22 7RU
0372 376161

Industrial Safety (Protective Equipment) Manufacturers
Association (ISPEMA)
69 Cannon Street
London EC4N 5AB
01-248 4444

Royal Society for the Prevention of Accidents
(ROSPA)
The Priory
Queensway
Birmingham B4 6BS
021-233 2461

British Safety Council
62-64 Chancellors Road
London W6 9RS
01-741 1231

Institute of Occupational Safety and Health (IOSH)
222 Uppingham Road
Leicester LE5 OQG
0533 768424

International Labour Office (ILO)
96/98 Marsham Street
London SW1P 4LY
01-828 6401

Royal Society of Chemistry
Burlington House
Piccadilly
London W1V OBN
01-437 8656

Chartered Institute of Building Services
222 Balham High Road
London SW12 9BS
01-675 5211

TUC Centenary Institute of Occupational Medicine
London School of Hygiene and Tropical Medicine
Keppel Street
London WC1E 7HT
01-636 8636

Institute of Occupational Health
University of Birmingham
University Road West
PO Box 363
Birmingham B15 2TT
021-471 3600

British Standards Institute (BSI)
Linford Wood
Milton Keynes MK14 6LE
0908 320033

Access to substantial databases on chemical hazards
can be gained via libraries and other organisations
equipped with the necessary computer search facilities.
HSE maintains HSELINE, a publicly available
database of references on all aspects of occupational
health and safety. For information on how to access
HSELINE contact:

Department of Trade and Industry
IRS/Dialtech
Room 392, Ashdown House
123 Victoria Street
London SW1E 6RB
01-212 5638

or

Pergamon Infoline
12 Vandy Street
London EC2A 2DE
01-377 4650

or

Datastar Marketing Ltd
Plaza Suite
114 Jermyn Street
London SW1Y 6HJ
01-930 5503

or

HSE Library and Information Services
Broad Lane
Sheffield S3 7HQ
0742 768141

As a further example the British Libraries BLAISE-LINK Service, 2 Sheraton Street, London W1V 4BH, telephone 01-636 1544, gives access to several databases including:

(a) TOXLINE - information on toxicology and environmental effects of chemicals; and

(b) CHEMLINE - information on chemicals

Some universities and many private companies provide an environmental monitoring and occupational hygiene service.

The HSC Newsletter and the Toxic Substances Bulletin are available by subscription from

Health and Safety Executive (HSE)
St Hugh's House
Stanley Precinct
Bootle L20 3QY

References

1 *Patty's Industrial Hygiene and Toxicology* J Wiley & Sons, 3rd edition
Vol 1, Ed. G D Clayton, F A Patty et al, ISBN 0471 16046 6
Vol 2A, Ed. G D and F E Clayton, ISBN 0471 16042 3
Vol 2B, Ed. G D and F E Clayton, ISBN 0471 07943 X
Vol 2C, Ed. G D and F E Clayton, ISBN 0471 09258 4
Vol 3, Ed. L J and L V Cralley, ISBN 0471 02698 0

2 *Casarett and Doull's Toxicology: The Basic Science of Poisons* C D Klaassen, M O Amdur et al, Macmillan Publishing Co Inc, 3rd edition 1986 ISBN 0 02 364650 0

3 *Dangerous Properties of Industrial Materials* N Irving Sax, Van Nostrand Reinhold Company, 6th edition 1984, ISBN 0442 28304 0

4 *Chemicals in the Printing Industry* British Printing Industries Federation (1980), ISBN 0 85168 128 X

5 *Safety in the Use of Isocyanate Pre-Polymers in the Printing and Printed Packaging Industries* Printing Industry Advisory Committee, HMSO, ISBN 0 11 883847 4

6 HSE Toxicity Review, No 9, 1,1,1-trichloroethane, HMSO, ISBN 0 11 883747 8

7 HSE Toxicity Review, No 10, Glycol Ethers, HMSO, ISBN 0 11 883807 5

8 Technical Reports Nos 4 and 17 on glycol ethers European Chemical Industry Ecology and Toxicology Centre (ECETOC) Brussels, Belgium

9 *Ink Fly in Newspaper Pressrooms* Printing Industry Advisory Committee, HMSO, ISBN 0 11 883751 6

10 *Occupational Skin Diseases: Health and Safety Precautions* HSE Guidance Note EH26, HMSO, ISBN 0 11 883374 X

11 *Safety in the Use of Inks, Varnishes and Lacquers Cured by Ultra-Violet Light* Printing Industry Advisory Committee, HSMO, ISBN 0 11 883678 1

12 *Occupational Exposure Limits* HSE Guidance Note EH40, HMSO, (reprinted annually), ISBN 0 11 883929 2

13 *Toxic Substances: A Precautionary Policy* HSE Guidance Note EH18, HMSO, ISBN 0 11 883178 X

14 *Writing a Safety Policy Statement: Advice to Employers* Health and Safety Commission, HSC6 (revised), available from HSE Offices

15 *Making your Safety Policy Work: The Implementation of Safety Policies in Printing Works* Printing Industry Advisory Committee leaflet, IAC/L14, available from HSE Offices

16 *The Provision of Health and Safety Information by Manufacturers, Importers and Suppliers of Chemical Products to the Printing Industry* Printing Industry Advisory Committee, HMSO, ISBN 0 11 883852 0

17 *Substances for Use at Work: The Provision of Information* Health and Safety series booklet HS(G)27, HMSO, ISBN 0 11 883844 X

18 *A Guide to the Classification, Packaging and Labelling of Dangerous Substances Regulations 1984* Health and Safety series booklet HS(R)22, HMSO, ISBN 0 11 883794 X

19 *Industrial Ventilation: A Manual of Recommended Practice* American Conference of Governmental Industrial Hygienists, ed. A Arbor, Edwards Brothers, Michigan, 19th edition, ISBN 0936 71265 1.
An Introduction to Local Exhaust Ventilation, Health and Safety series booklet HS(G)37, HMSO, ISBN 0 11 883954 3

20 *Ozone: Health Hazards and Precautionary Measures* HSE Guidance Note EH38, HMSO, ISBN 0 11 883562 9

21 *Certificate of Approval (Respiratory Protective Equipment)* Form 2486, published annually, HMSO, ISBN 0 11 883876 8

22 *Recommendations for the Selection, Use and Maintenance of Respiratory Protective Equipment* British Standard 4275 (1974), ISBN 0 580 08383 7

23 *Specification for Industrial Eye-Protectors* British Standard 2092 (1967)

24 *Planning Programme for the Prevention and Control of Fire in the Printing Industry* British Printing Industries Federation, ISBN 0 85168 098 4

25 Certificate of Approval No 1 (Form 2434), HMSO, ISBN 11 360640 0

26 *Code of Practice for the Selection, Installation and Maintenance of Electrical Apparatus for Use in Potentially Explosive Atmospheres* British Standard 5345, Part 1, ISBN 0 580 09414 6 and Part 2, ISBN 0 580 11954 8

27 *Electrical Apparatus for Use in Potentially Explosive Atmospheres* Health and Safety series booklet HS(G)22, HMSO, ISBN 0 11 883746 X

28 *The Storage of Highly Flammable Liquids,* HSE Guidance Note CS2, HMSO ISBN 0 11 883027 9

29 *Evaporating and Other Ovens* Health and Safety series booklet HS(G)16, HMSO, ISBN 0 11 883433 9

30 *Flame Arrestors and Explosion Reliefs* Health and Safety series booklet HS(G)11, HMSO, ISBN 0 11 883258 1

31 *Generation and Control of Static Electricity where Flammable Liquids are Stored and Used* Paintmakers Association of Great Britain

32 *Code of Practice for Control of Undesirable Static Electricity* British Standard 5958 Part 1 (1980), ISBN 0 580 11481 3

33 *The Keeping of LPG in Cylinders and Similar Containers* HSE Guidance Note CS4, HMSO, ISBN 0 11 883539 4

34 *The Storage of LPG at Fixed Installations* HSE Guidance Note CS5, HMSO, ISBN 0 11 883385 5

35 *Gaseous Fire Extinguishing Systems: Precautions for Toxic and Asphyxiating Hazards* HSE Guidance Note GS16, HMSO, ISBN 0 11 883574 2

36 *Storage of Packaged Dangerous Substances* HSE Guidance Note CS17, HMSO, ISBN 0 11 883526 2

37 *Dangerous Chemicals: Emergency Spillage Guide* Edited by P J Warren, Wolters Samson (UK) Ltd, 1985, ISBN 0 900319 39 9

38 *A Guide to the Notification of Installations Handling Hazardous Substances Regulations 1982* Health and Safety series booklet HS(R)16, HMSO, ISBN 0 11 883675 7

39 *A Guide to the Control of Industrial Major Accident Hazards Regulations 1984* Health and Safety series booklet HS(R)21, HMSO, ISBN 0 11 883767 2

40 *Entry into Confined Spaces* HSE Guidance Note GS5, HMSO, ISBN 0 11 883067 8

41 *The Cleaning and Gas Freeing of Tanks Containing Flammable Residues* HSE Guidance Note CS15, HMSO, ISBN 0 11 883518 1

42 *Asbestos in Paper and Board Mills* Paper and Board Industry Advisory Committee leaflet, IAC/L12, available free from HSE Offices

43 *First Aid at Work* Health and Safety series booklet HS(R)11, HMSO, ISBN 0 11 883446 0

44 *A Guide to The Safety Signs Regulations 1980* Health and Safety series booklet HS(R)7, HMSO, ISBN 0 11 883415 0

45 *Safety Signs and Colours* British Standard 5378 Part 1: ISBN 0 580 11506 2, Part 2: ISBN 0 580 11507 0, Part 3: ISBN 0 580 12779 0

46 *Reporting an Injury or a Dangerous Occurrence* HSE11 (Rev), available from HSE Offices

47 *Reporting a Case of Disease* HSE17, available from HSE Offices

48 *A Guide to the Reporting of Injuries, Diseases and Dangerous Occurrences Regulations 1985* Health and Safety series booklet HS(R)23, HMSO, ISBN 0 11 883858 X

Printing Industry Advisory Committee publications

Safety in Newspaper Production HSC, HMSO, ISBN 0 11 883677 3

Safety in the Use of Inks, Varnishes and Lacquers Cured by Ultra-violet Light HSC, HMSO, ISBN 0 11 883678 1

Ink Fly in Newspaper Pressrooms HSC, HMSO, ISBN 0 11 883751 6

Safety in the Use of Isocyanate Prepolymers in the Printing and Printed Packaging Industries HSC, HMSO, ISBN 0 11 883847 4

The Provision of Health and Safety Information by Manufacturers, Importers and Suppliers of Chemical Products to the Printing Industry HSC, HMSO, ISBN 0 11 883852 0

Making your Safety Policy Work: The Implementation of Safety Policies in Printing Works HSC, IAC/L14, available free from HSE offices

Noise Reduction at Buckle Folding Machines HSC, HMSO, ISBN 0 11 883849 0

Health and Safety for Small Firms in the Print Industry HSC, HMSO, ISBN 0 11 883851 2

Control of Lead in the Printing Industry HSC, IAC/L24, available free from HSE offices

Printed in the United Kingdom for Her Majesty's Stationery Office
Dd 289611 C45 11/87 (40711)